D O G

T R E A T S

D O G

T R E A T S

Kim Campbell Thornton

Illustrations by Mark Matcho

Main Street Books
Doubleday

New York
London
Toronto
Sydney
Auckland

A MAIN STREET BOOK
PUBLISHED BY DOUBLEDAY

a division of Bantam Doubleday Dell Publishing Group, Inc.
1540 Broadway, New York, New York 10036

MAIN STREET BOOKS, DOUBLEDAY, and the portrayal of a building with a tree are trademarks
of Doubleday, a division of Bantam Doubleday Dell Publishing Group, Inc.

Design by Amanda Kavanagh, ARK design
Images of dog, fur and tablecloth © 1996 PhotoDisc, Inc.

Library of Congress Cataloging-in-Publication Data
Thornton, Kim Campbell.
    Dog treats / Kim Campbell Thornton.—1st Main Street books ed.
        p.   cm.
    "Main Street books."
    1. Dogs—Food—Recipes.   2. Dogs—Nutrition.   3. Dogs.   I. Title.
SF427.4.T48   1997
636.7'0852—dc21   96-52018
                                                       CIP

ISBN 0-385-48460-7
Copyright © 1997 Kim Campbell Thornton
Printed in the United States of America
October 1997
First Edition
10 9 8 7 6 5 4 3 2 1

To Savanna, the best dog a cook could ever have.

Acknowledgments

My deepest thanks go to John Hamil, DVM, who vetted the health and nutrition information in this book; and to recipe testers (and tasters) Liz Palika and Australian shepherds Care Bear, Ursa, and Dax; Alex and Siberian husky Sibu; Rocky Guidry; Ellyce Kaluf, Audrey Pavia, Betsy Siino, and Chris Walkowicz; and, of course, my greyhound Savanna, who will eat anything. Thanks also to Vicki Baldwin at The Scoop for permission to reprint certain recipes.

Contents

Author's Note

When I was first asked to write this book, I wasn't sure what my answer should be. After all, as editor of *Dog Fancy* magazine, it had always been my policy to recommend that dog owners feed only a commercial diet that was balanced and complete, avoiding table scraps. However, I knew from my mail that most owners enjoy giving their pet "people food" and believe that it is important for them to have variety in their diets. Most veterinary nutritionists would argue with that concept, but the fact remains that people love their dogs and want to do special things for them, including feeding treats.

This book is written for them. With a foundation of a well-balanced diet and careful calorie counting, there's no harm in providing the occasional special meal or homemade treat, especially if it is formulated with a dog's dietary needs in mind. So the next time you're feeling creative (or hungry), consider whipping up something in the kitchen for Rover as well. You'll both enjoy the experience.

Introduction

It's the great debate: Should dogs eat people food, or should owners feed a commercially prepared food that is complete and balanced? Is a homemade diet prepared with fresh food more nutritious than commercial food? Do dogs need vitamin and mineral supplements to be healthy? With the current interest in a wholesome lifestyle, these are just a few of the questions that concern today's health-conscious dog owner.

Diet and nutrition are topics of hot debate among veterinary nutritionists, pet owners, and dog breeders. Among the theories being discussed in veterinary circles are the benefits of caloric restriction to increase lifespan, the use of antioxidant vitamins to fight cellular aging, and the addition of fatty-acid supplements to the diet. Ask ten different people what they think dogs should eat, and you will get ten different answers. The food that is best for an individual dog can depend on the dog's age, breed, size, health, and lifestyle.

Just as people are individuals and have individual nutritional needs, so do dogs. The canine couch potato will develop behavioral problems if fed the same high-energy diet needed by a working dog. Some dogs are more prone to obesity than others and must be kept on a strict feeding schedule or fed a low-calorie food. Growing puppies require more calories than adults, but too many calories can cause skeletal development problems.

Pet food manufacturers have responded to canine nutritional needs by developing foods for every life stage and lifestyle. There are foods for puppies, foods for adult dogs, foods for old dogs, foods for fat dogs. Veterinarians can prescribe therapeutic diets for dogs with heart disease, kidney problems, and digestive disorders. Owners of hard-working hunting or sled dogs can choose from a variety of high-protein diets. Female dogs that are pregnant or producing milk for their pups also require a higher protein diet than the average household dog.

Whatever the case, most veterinary experts agree that a high-quality canned or dry commercial food is the best diet for a dog whose owner does not have the time or inclination to develop a balanced diet and cook it regularly for the dog. This is the case in most of today's busy two-earner households. Canned food is extremely palatable, and dry food helps keep teeth clean and tartar-free. Manufacturers use ingredients that provide complete and balanced nutrition, and many test their foods' nutritional quality and palatability with feeding trials, in which a number of different types of dogs are fed the diet.

Nevertheless, studies show that dogs enjoy eating new or unusual foods. For the dog that enjoys treats—and the owner who enjoys cooking—there is no harm and much fun in providing occasional homemade treats or even entire meals. Special occasions such as holidays or the dog's birthday can be opportunities for home-cooked meals, as can a weekend ritual, such as Sunday breakfast together or an afternoon picnic after a hike.

The following recipes in most cases can be shared by dog and owner. They have been adapted for canine tastes and nutritional requirements, and are generally low in fat to help prevent excessive calorie intake, but with minor adjustments for seasoning and temperature to human portions, people can enjoy them too (the exceptions being such dogs-only items as Chocolate Lab Liver-Chip Brownies and the various biscuit, bread, and cookie items). The amount you serve should be proportional to your dog's size. One to two tablespoons is plenty for a toy breed, and one cup is appropriate for a dog that weighs fifty pounds or more. Why the small serving size? Dogs tend to have sensitive digestive tracts. Too much of a new or rich food can cause diarrhea. Another reason is to prevent your dog from developing a preference for the treat meal and refusing his regular food. Restricting a dog's intake will benefit you both. By reserving treats for special occasions, you keep them just that: special!

*Your Dog's
Nutritional Needs*

CHAPTER 1

Dogs and cats are not little people in fur suits, nor are they alike in their dietary needs. Each species has individual nutritional requirements based on its anatomic, behavioral, and metabolic evolution. Both belong to the order Carnivora, so many people assume that the canine diet, like that of the feline, must be meat-based. However, a dog's digestive system is capable of utilizing plant sources of nutrition as well, making it *omnivorous*. Dogs have lower protein requirements than cats, and their bodies are built for efficient use of carbohydrates as well as synthesis from plants of such essential nutrients as vitamin A and niacin. However, meat contains all the essential amino acids a dog needs in its diet, so it is an important part of dog food. And the canine digestive system, from the teeth to the intestines, is built to process meat quickly so the body can make use of it.

Water: The Life-Giving Liquid

Be sure your dog always has a supply of fresh, clean water along with its food. No other nutrient is as important to dogs as water. Dogs can survive for days without food, but without water they will die quickly. That's because water makes up about 60 percent of an adult dog's body, with the percentage being even higher in puppies. Water is at the heart of bodily processes. Cells can't function without water, and water acts as a lubricant for tissues throughout the body. The body loses water through urination, defecation, lactation, respiration, and panting, diarrhea, and vomiting. That's why fluid replacement is especially important when a dog is sick or when it has been exerting itself.

In addition to regular water intake, the body absorbs water from food and from the metabolic processing of carbohydrates, fats, and proteins. The amount of water a dog drinks depends on the type of food it eats. Because canned food contains a large amount of water, dogs that eat primarily canned food will drink less water than those on a dry diet.

You may want to give your dog the same bottled water you drink yourself. Bottled water has many health benefits compared to tap water, which is not always guaranteed to be clean and safe, according to the Environmental Protection Agency and the Centers for Disease Control. High levels of lead, nitrates, and herbicides have been found in the drinking water of some areas of the United States. Tap water can also contain parasites and other contaminants. To safeguard his patients' health, one holistic veterinarian recommends that his clients give their pets filtered or bottled water. For a special treat, give your dog one of the many flavored bottled waters manufactured especially for pets.

Hint

If you take your dog on a cross-country trip or move to a new city, be sure to bring along a gallon or two of water from home. Mix the dog's regular water with the water in the new area to minimize digestive upsets.

Biscuits, Breads,
and Cookies

CHAPTER 2

Just about everyone has a favorite recipe for dog biscuits or cookies. Hard biscuits are not only treats; they also serve a healthful purpose, by helping to scrape tartar off your dog's teeth. The cookie recipes are developed specially for dogs with little of the fat and sugar found in the cookies people eat. Collected here are many traditional favorites such as liver- and cheese-flavored biscuits, as well as some new variations on an old theme.

Wheaten Milk Biscuits

The milk biscuit is a canine classic. Puppies cut their teeth on them, and adult dogs relish the crunchy treats.

1/2 cup wheat germ
1/2 cup powdered milk
1 cup all-purpose flour
1 cup whole-wheat flour
6 tablespoons butter-flavored shortening
1 egg
1 teaspoon brown sugar
1/2 cup water

The soft-coated wheaten terrier is a medium-size Irish breed with a bearded face and a lively temperament. His soft, silky coat can be any shade from light wheaten to reddish gold.

Preheat oven to 325°. Combine dry ingredients. Cut in shortening until crumbly. Beat egg and combine with brown sugar. Add to flour mixture. Gradually add water until a stiff dough is formed. Knead until smooth and pliable. Roll out dough to 1/2-inch thickness and cut into the classic bone shape. Bake for 30 minutes. Store in refrigerator.

2 cups brown rice flour
1 tablespoon activated charcoal
    (available at the drugstore)
1 large egg, lightly beaten
3 tablespoons vegetable oil
$1/2$ cup chopped parsley
$1/3$ cup chopped fresh mint
$2/3$ cup milk

Boom Boom's Breath Bars

Could your dog's breath knock Arnold Schwarzenegger flat? Try sweetening it with these biscuits, which contain charcoal, parsley, and mint to fight bad breath. The hard texture will help remove tartar buildup.

Hint

Preheat oven to 400°. Grease baking sheet. Combine flour and charcoal. In another bowl, combine the egg, oil, parsley, and mint, and mix well. Gradually stir in the flour mixture, and add enough milk to make a dough the consistency of drop biscuits. Drop heaping tablespoons of dough about one inch apart on the baking sheet. Bake 15 minutes, or until firm. Store the cooled biscuits in a tightly covered container in the refrigerator.

Don't brush Boom Boom's teeth with Crest or any other toothpaste formulated for people. The ingredients can cause stomach upset. To keep your dog's teeth really clean, brush them daily or weekly with a toothpaste made for dogs and schedule annual veterinary cleanings.

7

Cheesy Garlic Biscuits

Cheese and garlic are two favorite dog flavors. Don't be surprised if your dog smells them baking and stakes out the kitchen, waiting impatiently for them to come out of the oven.

2 cups whole-wheat flour
1 cup cheddar cheese, grated
2 tablespoons margarine or
    shortening
¾ cup milk
garlic powder

Did you know . . . ? A dog has a sense of smell that is one to two million times greater than that of a human. The incredible canine nose is used to help find lost people and detect drugs, bombs, and evidence of arson. The bloodhound is especially noted for its scenting ability.

Preheat oven to 375°. Combine flour and cheese, and cut in margarine or shortening. Add milk and mix well. Knead lightly. Divide dough into two parts, and roll out to 1-inch thickness on a floured board. Cut into desired shapes, and place biscuits on an ungreased cookie sheet. Prick with a fork, and sprinkle with garlic powder. Bake 12 to 15 minutes, or until lightly browned. Cool and serve. Refrigerate to store.

Pal's Peanut Butter 'n' Raisin Biscuits

Most dogs love peanut butter, so this biscuit recipe is sure to be a hit.

1½ cups whole-wheat flour

½ cup wheat germ

1 tablespoon brown sugar

1¼ cups smooth peanut butter

¾ cup milk

¼ cup raisins

Preheat oven to 400°. Combine flour, wheat germ, and sugar in mixing bowl. Place peanut butter and milk in a separate bowl and blend well with an electric mixer. Pour peanut-butter mixture and raisins into dry ingredients and mix well. Turn dough out onto a lightly floured board and knead lightly. Roll out ¼-inch thick and cut into desired shapes. Place biscuits about ½ inch apart on baking sheet, and bake for 15 minutes, or until slightly browned. Refrigerate or freeze until use.

Did you know . . . ? The ten most popular names for dogs are Max, Lady, Jake, Molly and Sam (tied), Shadow, Buddy and Ginger (tied), Casey, Sadie, Maggie, and Buster.

9

Pooch Pizza

Does your dog beg for a piece of your pepperoni pizza? Give him something a little less spicy with these pizza-flavored biscuits.

3 cups whole-wheat flour
1 cup oats, uncooked
1 cup Parmesan, mozzarella, or
    Romano cheese, grated
2 tablespoons margarine or
    shortening
1 egg, beaten
$^2/_3$ cup canned tomato sauce
$^1/_3$ cup water
olive oil
garlic powder

Hint

To keep your dog occupied while you are away from home, stuff a Kong toy or other hollow, sturdy toy with peanut butter, soft cheese, or small treats. Your dog will spend hours trying to get at the goodies!

Combine flour, oats, and cheese, and cut in margarine or shortening. Add egg, tomato sauce, and water, and mix well. Knead lightly, then refrigerate for 1 hour. When dough is chilled, preheat oven to 375°. Divide dough into two parts, and roll out to 1-inch thickness on a floured board. Cut into rounds or triangles, and place biscuits on an ungreased cookie sheet. Prick with a fork, brush with olive oil, and sprinkle with garlic powder. Bake 10 to 12 minutes, or until lightly browned. Let cool and serve. Store in refrigerator.

1 cup whole-wheat flour

3/4 cup nonfat dry milk powder

1/2 cup rolled oats

1/4 cup cornmeal

2 teaspoons chicken bouillon
   granules

1/3 cup shortening

1 egg

1/2 cup hot water

Combine dry ingredients, and cut in shortening until mixture resembles coarse crumbs. Add egg and stir. Then add hot water and stir until dough is the consistency of drop biscuit batter. Drop dough by the tablespoon on a flat microwave-safe dish. Microwave at 50 percent for 8 to 10 minutes, rotating plate every 2 minutes. Turn cookies halfway through the cooking process. They should be firm and dry to the touch when done. Let cool before serving. Cookies will harden as they cool.

Chicken-Flavored Microwave Cookies

This cookie recipe is a good one to make in the summertime, since a microwave won't heat up the kitchen the way an oven will. They're not bad, with a flavor like Chicken in a Biskit crackers.

Hint

Withhold food for several hours before shipping your dog by air. That way, turbulence is less likely to cause stomach upset. It also minimizes your dog's need to defecate, which can be important on a long trip. To prevent dehydration, place ice cubes in the water dish. They won't spill the way water can, thus providing a longer-lasting source of water.

West Highland Oatmeal Cookies

Offer these oatmeal delights to your Westie, Scottie, cairn terrier, Scottish deerhound, or Gordon setter. But even if you don't own a Scottish breed, your dog is sure to enjoy them.

$3/4$ cup oatmeal

$3/4$ cup whole-wheat or rye flour

2 tablespoons wheat germ

2 tablespoons brown sugar

1 5-ounce can evaporated milk

2 tablespoons butter or margarine, melted

2 tablespoons honey

Great Britain is where a number of great breeds were developed. It is home to all the terrier breeds save the schnauzers as well as to many of the sporting and hound breeds such as the golden retriever, the English and Welsh springer spaniels, the English foxhound, the beagle, and the otter hound.

Combine dry ingredients. Add remaining ingredients (pour the honey into the measuring cup you used to melt the butter—it will pour out faster). Blend well to make a stiff dough. Chill dough for a half hour. Preheat oven to 350°. Roll teaspoons of dough into balls, flatten, and place on a greased cookie sheet. Bake 12 to 15 minutes, or until done. Refrigerate or freeze to store.

12

1 package dry yeast
$1/3$ cup warm water
$3^{1}/_{2}$ cups all-purpose flour
2 cups whole-wheat flour
2 cups oatmeal
1 cup rye flour
1 cup cornmeal
$1/2$ cup nonfat dry milk
1 pint chicken or beef broth
1 egg
1 tablespoon milk

Preheat oven to 300°. Dissolve yeast in warm water (about 110°). Combine dry ingredients and add yeast mixture and broth. Turn out onto a floured board and knead well, about 3 minutes, forming a stiff dough. Divide dough in half and roll out to $1/4$-inch thickness. Cut out into desired shapes and place on greased cookie sheet. Mix egg and 1 tablespoon milk to make a glaze; brush on biscuits. Bake 45 minutes. Turn off oven and let harden overnight. Yield: up to 200 biscuits.

Party Biscuits

When you're expecting a crowd, this is the recipe to use. Consider making these biscuits to sell at a bake sale to raise money for your local animal shelter or dog club, or give them to dog-owning friends at the holidays.

Dogs have helped farmers for centuries, serving as herding dogs, flock guards, and even cattle drivers. The rottweiler was once known as the butcher's dog, because it took the cattle to market and then brought the money back home around its neck.

Say Chicken-Cheese!

These tasty cookies contain two favorite dog flavors.

3/4 cup wheat germ

3/4 cup whole-wheat flour

1 jar chicken baby food

1/2 cup cheddar cheese

1/2 baby-food jar water

3/4 cup powdered milk

1 egg

Believe it or not, there's a breed called the Danish chicken dog. This medium-size brown and white dog is an all-around farm helper. He is found only in Denmark, not in the United States.

Preheat oven to 350°. Combine ingredients and mix thoroughly. Drop teaspoons of dough onto an ungreased cookie sheet. Bake 20 minutes. Store in refrigerator if cookies are to be used within a few days; otherwise, freeze them in small batches.

¾ cup all-purpose flour

¾ cup whole-wheat flour

1 cup sharp cheddar, grated

4 tablespoons butter-flavored
    shortening

1 egg

½ cup buttermilk

2 apples, peeled, cored, and grated
    or chopped finely

1 teaspoon fresh parsley, chopped

Preheat oven to 400°. Combine flours
and cheese, and cut in shortening.
Beat egg with buttermilk, and pour
into flour mixture. Add apples and
parsley to wet flour mixture, and stir
until a soft dough forms. Drop by the
tablespoon onto an ungreased cookie
sheet, and bake 15 to 20 minutes.

Herbed Cheese-
Apple Cookies

The sweetness of apples, savory flavor
of cheddar, and fresh taste of parsley all
combine to make this a doggone delicious cookie.

Hint

*Look for novelty cookie cutters in cook-
ware and pet-supply stores and catalogs.
If you can't find a bone-shaped biscuit
cutter, make a cardboard pattern of a
dog bone by tracing a store-bought dog
biscuit. Place the pattern on top of the
rolled-out dough and cut around it.*

15

Piper's Peanut Butter Sandwich

Hint

If your dog doesn't like to take pills, disguise them by hiding them inside a soft treat or covering them with peanut butter or cream cheese.

Spread peanut butter on one small or medium-size dog biscuit (depending on your dog's size). Top with another biscuit and serve. This quick and easy treat will satisfy your dog for several minutes as he works to get every last bit of the peanut butter off the roof of his mouth!

2 cups whole wheat flour

1/3 cup butter, melted

1 egg, beaten

6 tablespoons water

1/4 to 1/2 cup dried liver bits or jerky-
style treats, chopped

Chocolate Lab Liver-Chip Cookies

Chocolate isn't good for your dog, but that doesn't mean he can't have his own special version of chocolate chip cookies. Just don't get them mixed up with your own!

Preheat oven to 350°. Combine flour, butter, egg, and water. Mix well. Blend in liver bits. Turn onto a greased baking pan. Bake 20 to 25 minutes. Cool and cut.

The Labrador retriever is America's most popular breed, prized for its versatility as a hunter, guide dog, drug detector, and just plain buddy. The Labrador comes in three colors: black, yellow, and, of course, chocolate.

Breakfast with Bowser

CHAPTER 3

1 tablespoon butter
2 eggs, beaten
1/4 cup dry cottage cheese

Setter Scramble

Scrambled eggs are healthy as well as easy to fix. They take only two to three minutes to prepare and cook. Offer them to pique the appetite of a dog who isn't feeling well. Scrambled eggs are bland and smooth, and should sit well on an upset tummy.

Hint

Melt the butter in a frying pan, and remove from heat. Combine beaten eggs and cottage cheese, and pour into frying pan. Return pan to low heat, and stir the egg mixture with a fork until set. Serve separately or over the dog's regular food.

Dogs should always be fed cooked, not raw, eggs because raw egg whites interfere with the absorption of biotin, one of the B vitamins. Raw eggs also carry the danger of salmonella poisoning.

19

Chesapeake Cheese Omelet

1½ tablespoons butter
1 tablespoon dry bread crumbs
2 eggs, beaten
4 tablespoons cheddar cheese, grated

Famed as a duck dog, the Chesapeake Bay retriever is one of ten American Kennel Club breeds "made in the USA." Its dense, harsh coat, which ranges in color from "deadgrass" to liver or hay, allows it to shake off wetness like water off a duck's back. This is a hard-headed breed that likes nothing better than to retrieve all day, even in wet, icy conditions.

Heat butter in pan over medium heat. Mix bread crumbs with eggs, and pour into pan. When omelet is almost cooked, add cheddar over half of it, and fold over the other half. Continue cooking 3 minutes, until cheese melts. Let cool and serve.

2 cups milk

1/4 cup brown sugar

1 tablespoon butter

1/4 teaspoon salt

1/4 teaspoon cinnamon

1 cup rolled oats

1 cup apple, peeled, cored, and
    chopped

1/2 cup raisins

Apple-Raisin Oatmeal

This makes a great winter-morning breakfast before playing in the snow.

Combine milk, brown sugar, butter, salt, and cinnamon in an ovenproof pot and bring to a boil. Remove pot from heat and stir in oats, apple, and raisins. Bring mixture to a simmer, place pot in oven, and cook uncovered 30 minutes. Let cool and serve. Makes 4 to 8 servings, depending on number of people and size of dogs.

Did you know . . . ? Vitamins are either fat-soluble (A, D, E, and K) or water-soluble (B and C). The body stores excess fat-soluble vitamins, which can lead to toxicity if too much builds up, but excess water-soluble vitamins are eliminated in the urine.

Hound Dog Delight

This cheesy soufflé-type dish is good for breakfast or dinner. People will want additional seasoning.

2½ cups water
½ cup grits
½ teaspoon salt
3 eggs, beaten
½ cup cheddar cheese, grated
2 cloves garlic, chopped

The black-and-tan coonhound was developed in America to tree the raccoon, an animal new to immigrants from Europe. Today, coonhounds still test their prowess against the wily raccoon, but once the coon is treed, honor is satisfied and everyone goes home for dinner—even the raccoon!

Preheat oven to 400°. Bring water to a boil, and slowly stir in grits and salt. Cook until done, about 3 minutes for quick grits, 15 minutes for regular grits. Remove from heat and stir in eggs, cheese, and garlic. Pour into deep, greased baking dish, and bake 30 minutes. Cool to room temperature and serve. Refrigerate leftovers.

1/4 cup water
1/4 cup raisins
2 tablespoons honey
2 cups cooked brown or white rice
8 ounces plain yogurt or cottage
   cheese

Ridgeback Rice Pudding

This is a good choice for a dog that has an upset stomach or diarrhea. The bland, soothing pudding is good canine "comfort food."

Combine water, raisins, and honey in a 1-quart saucepan, and bring to a boil. Stir in rice and let cool. Fold in yogurt or cottage cheese, and serve warm or chilled. Refrigerate leftovers.

European settlers in the African land once called Rhodesia (now Zambia and Zimbabwe) created the Rhodesian Ridgeback to hunt lions, and it was originally known as the Rhodesian lion dog. This powerful breed is distinguished by the ridge of hair that grows along the center of its back. The owner of a Ridgeback must be prepared to give it plenty of exercise and training to keep it occupied.

Hush Puppies

These treats have long been favorites in the South. The story goes that hunters used to quiet their dogs by tossing them pieces of fried corn dough and saying, "Hush, puppy!" Your dog, Southern or not, will enjoy this updated version of a treat enjoyed by dogs for decades.

1 cup cornmeal
$^1/_3$ cup thawed frozen corn or mixed vegetables; fresh, whole corn kernels; or canned corn, drained
$^3/_4$ cup grated cheddar cheese
$^1/_2$ cup plus 2 tablespoons milk

Did you know . . . ? Fat is a concentrated energy source that provides vitamins A, D, E, and K and essential fatty acids, as well as helping make food taste good. On the downside, when too much energy is stored as fat, which occurs when a dog eats too much on a regular basis, the result is obesity, the cause of numerous health problems.

Preheat oven to 425°. In a bowl, combine cornmeal, corn, and cheese. Make a well in the center and add milk, stirring only until combined. Drop batter by the tablespoon onto greased cookie sheet. Bake 15 minutes, or until golden brown. Let cool before serving. Makes 10 to 12 hush puppies. Refrigerate to store.

2 ounces frozen orange juice
    concentrate
5 ounces acidophilus, soy, or rice milk
5 crushed ice cubes

Orange Slushpuppy

My dog Savanna loves oranges and can smell one being peeled from the back of the house. She thinks this slush is pretty good, too. This frothy drink is a cool refresher on a hot day. You can also pour the orange slush into ice cube trays and freeze to make "pupsicles."

Place orange juice, milk, and ice in blender, and beat on high for 1 minute. Serve. For a change of pace, you can substitute one frozen banana or a half cup of frozen strawberries or peaches for the orange juice.

Did you know . . . ? Your dog's liver produces all the vitamin C he needs, so it is not necessary in the diet, although extra vitamin C may benefit working dogs or dogs with liver disease. Vitamin C supplements may also be useful for dogs recovering from surgery. Since excess vitamin C is eliminated from the body, there's no danger of the dog getting too much.

Yogurt Pupsicles

These are just the thing for a hot summer day. You and your dog can enjoy them together as you laze the day away.

1 pint plain nonfat yogurt
$1/2$ small can (3 ounces) frozen orange juice concentrate

Hint

Young puppies should eat four meals a day. As they grow, they can be switched to two meals daily. Be sure to ration your puppy's intake. Rapid growth, especially in large breeds, can impair skeletal development.

Combine ingredients and mix well. Freeze in ice cube trays. Serve.

2 tablespoons oats

¹/₂ banana, mashed

1 4-ounce container plain yogurt

¹/₂ cup orange juice

¹/₂ apple, peeled, cored, and chopped

¹/₂ cup berries in season

Great Grrrnola

Most dogs love fruit and yogurt and will find this healthy cereal appealing. So will you!

Mix oats and banana, blending well. Add yogurt, orange juice, and apple. Mash berries and add to mixture. Serve in small portions; too much fruit can cause diarrhea in a digestive system that is un-used to it.

Toby, a Boston terrier in Zephyr Hills, Florida, likes to peel and eat his own or-anges. Valencia oranges are his favorite.

Soups, Stews, and Sauces

CHAPTER 4

Warm, hearty soups and stews will help keep your dog toasty during the cold winter months. If your dog spends much time outdoors during winter, he will appreciate having his regular food topped with an occasional serving of these delicious high-protein meals.

Bulldog Beef Stew

Beef and vegetables are a quintessentially British combination, so it's appropriate to name this stew after England's symbol: the bulldog.

1 pound beef stew meat, cubed
2 large carrots, chopped
1 large potato, cubed (leave skin on)
2 cloves garlic, chopped
2 cups water
2 tablespoons fresh parsley, chopped

Many dog breeds were once raised as food sources in their native countries, including the chow chow, chihuahua, and Chinese crested. Today, both they and we are lucky that they serve only as companions, not cuisine!

Preheat oven to 275°. Place all ingredients in large pot and cover tightly. Bake 5 hours. This stew should need no attention, but you can check occasionally to make sure it isn't scorching. Add more water if necessary. When done, cool to room temperature and serve. Top with fresh parsley for added interest. Refrigerate leftovers.

1 15-ounce can garbanzo beans

1 tablespoon olive oil

2 cloves garlic, minced

2 cups mixed vegetables (use
   packaged mixed vegetables, or
   try celery, carrots, green beans,
   and zucchini)

1 potato, peeled and diced

2 tablespoons tomato paste

6 cups water

2 cups macaroni

Drain and rinse the garbanzo beans. Heat oil in a large pot over low heat and sauté garlic for 5 minutes. Add vegetables and potato, and cook for 5 minutes. Stir in tomato paste, then add garbanzo beans and water. Bring to a boil, cover, and simmer 55 minutes. Add macaroni and cook 5–8 minutes. Let cool and serve. Refrigerate leftovers.

Spinone Minestrone

This hearty vegetable stew is a good meal to share on a camping trip. The Italian Spinone is an all-purpose gundog that has been known in Italy for two thousand years.

Hint

When hiking or camping in wilderness areas, always bring a supply of clean water for your dog to drink. If you run out of water from home, boil or otherwise purify water from other sources. That clear stream or river hides *Giardia lamblia*, a parasite that can cause severe diarrhea in dogs and humans.

Cheddar-Tomato Sauce

Cheese and tomatoes are two favorite dog flavors. This sauce will tantalize your dog's taste buds.

1 can cheddar cheese soup
1 can tomato soup
1 soup can water or milk

Did you know . . . ? There are sound medical reasons for feeding your dog two to four small meals daily rather than a single large meal. Multiple meals can help prevent gastric torsion, or bloat, and they are recommended for hard-working dogs with high energy requirements such as sled dogs and hunting dogs, as well as puppies and pregnant or lactating females.

Cold soups are refreshing in summertime. When the temperature rises, let your dog chill out with this soup.

Stir together all ingredients and heat. Serve over dry dog food. Be sure it's not too hot.

1 avocado, mashed
1 can cream of chicken soup
$1/2$ to 1 cup plain yogurt

Rocky's Avocado Soup

Rocky's owner, Wayne, is lucky to harvest any of his avocados, because the big Rhodesian Ridgeback–Saint Bernard mix often beats him to them. This soup is easy to make, and Rocky enjoys it on hot San Diego days. Avocados are good for your dog's coat, too.

Hint

Place all ingredients in blender and mix well. Amount of yogurt depends on consistency you prefer. Serve at room temperature.

If your dog isn't eating, there are a number of possible causes. Hot weather, illness, or a change in diet can all put your dog off his feed. Sometimes, dogs just like to skip a meal. If Rover seems healthy otherwise, don't worry if he skips a meal or two, but if he is lethargic and continues to refuse to eat, take him to the veterinarian.

Pasta and Vegetables

CHAPTER 5

Dogs in Italy are accustomed to pasta, but it may be a new taste sensation for their American cousins. Whether you own a Bracco Italiano (an Italian pointing breed) or a Boston terrier, though, don't be surprised if your dog delights in a variety of noodle dishes.

Pomeranian Pasta Primavera

Celebrate spring with fresh vegetables and pasta. When I started preparing this, the whole gang—Savanna and the three cats—gathered in the kitchen, waiting with anticipatory relish. How they knew they were getting some I haven't figured out yet. They all ate their servings with gusto.

Hint

Broccoli can cause gas, so if your dog is prone to flatulence you may wish to substitute another vegetable.

When it was first bred in the German province of Pomerania, this spitz breed weighed up to thirty pounds. Today the Pomeranian has shrunk to three to seven pounds and stands only eleven inches high. Its fluffy coat comes in twelve colors or combinations of colors, and its curious, alert personality makes it a good alarm dog.

1 10-ounce package orzo (rice-shaped pasta), or the pasta of your choice (be sure it's something that will be easy for your dog to eat, such as shells, elbows, or rotini)

$1/2$ cup broccoli

$1/2$ cup carrots, chopped

$1/2$ cup zucchini, chopped

$1/2$ cup celery, chopped

2 cloves garlic, chopped

2 tablespoons olive oil

$1/2$ cup vegetable or chicken broth

Cook the orzo, drain, and set aside to cool. Lightly sauté the vegetables and garlic in the olive oil until they are crisply tender. Add broth and cook down briefly. Stir in the pasta, allow to cool, and serve at room temperature. Vary the vegetables according to what's available in your market or garden. Dogs also like fresh peas and asparagus.

- 1/3 cup vegetable oil
- 2 cloves garlic, chopped
- 1 pound ground beef
- 2 tomatoes, chopped
- 1 cup cottage cheese
- 1 pound macaroni, cooked and drained
- 1 cup Cheddar-Tomato Sauce (see page 32)

Neapolitan Macaroni and Beef Casserole

Real dogs do eat salad! It may never have occurred to you to give your dog fruits and vegetables, but most dogs love them and they make great low-calorie treats, especially for dogs on a diet. Frozen mixed vegetables are good hot-weather treats. The next time you're making a salad, don't leave Spike out of the preparations—toss him a couple of chopped carrot bits or broccoli florets and see what he thinks!

Hint

Preheat oven to 375°. Heat vegetable oil in skillet, and sauté garlic for 5 minutes. Add beef and brown. Add tomatoes, and cook over low heat for 15 minutes. Remove from heat and blend in cottage cheese. Spread half the macaroni on the bottom of a greased baking dish. Top with meat mixture, the remaining macaroni, and the Cheddar-Tomato Sauce. Bake for 35 minutes. Let cool and serve. Leftovers can be frozen.

Never give your dog onions. Cooked or raw onions, especially in large quantities, can cause anemia by destroying a dog's red blood cells.

Main Courses

CHAPTER 6

1 tablespoon vegetable oil
2 cups roast chicken, turkey, or beef, chopped
1 cup mixed vegetables
2 tablespoons parsley, chopped
1/2 cup gravy or nonfat yogurt
2 cups mashed potatoes

Australian Shepherd's Pie

Preheat oven to 400°. Heat oil in skillet. Add meat, vegetables (I use carrots, green beans, and butter beans), parsley, and gravy or yogurt, and cook over medium heat until browned, stirring frequently to prevent sticking. Spread in a pie pan and top with mashed potatoes, which can be hot or cold. Bake until potatoes are browned, about 20 minutes. Let cool and serve. Refrigerate leftovers.

Despite its name, the Australian shepherd is not from the land Down Under but was developed in America by Basque shepherds in the late nineteenth century. This active, busy breed is happiest when it has a job to do. One enterprising owner taught her Aussies to pick up dirty clothes around the house and bring them to the laundry room.

Catahoula Chicken and Rice

This is a favorite meal of both humans and animals in our house. It's easy to fix, and it tastes great!

1 tablespoon olive oil

1 cup rice

2 cups chopped tomatoes, canned or fresh

1 clove garlic, chopped

2 cups chicken, cubed

2 cups water or 1 15-ounce can nonfat, low-sodium chicken broth

Louisiana's Catahoula leopard dog is a tough breed that is used to work cattle and drive wild hogs. It is Louisiana's state dog and was developed from the mastiff-type dogs brought by Spanish explorers to America in the sixteenth century.

Heat olive oil in skillet. Sauté rice until golden, about 5 minutes. Add tomatoes, garlic, chicken, and water or broth. Bring to a simmer, cover, and cook on low heat for 20 minutes. Let cool and serve.

1 tablespoon peanut oil

1 cup diced chicken

1 clove garlic, crushed

1 teaspoon soy sauce

1½ cups diced zucchini or mixed
   vegetables

Chow Chow Chicken Stir-fry

Does your dog like to share your Chinese food? Make him his own with the following recipe. It will be lower in sodium and MSG than your regular Chinese takeout. It's so good you might want to try it yourself!

Heat oil in skillet or wok, and stir-fry chicken, garlic, and soy sauce over high heat. When chicken turns white, add zucchini or vegetables, cover, and cook 5 minutes. Let cool and serve alone or over rice. For a change of pace, try substituting celery for zucchini.

The chow chow, which once served in China not only as a draft and guard dog but also as dinner, is believed to have descended from spitz- and mastiff-type dogs. Its black tongue, lips, and gums are a hallmark of the breed.

Chicken Loaf Lhasa

Dogs love the taste of chicken. They will enjoy this loaf-style dish.

2 tablespoons vegetable oil
1½ pounds chicken legs or thighs
1 cup water
1½ cups mixed vegetables
1 can evaporated milk

The Lhasa apso was prized as a luck bringer in its homeland of Tibet, and it was not uncommon for the country's spiritual leader, the Dalai Lama, to present the Chinese imperial court with these dogs as a token of great esteem. The Lhasa's appearance earned it the sobriquet "lion dog."

Heat oil in skillet and brown chicken. Add water and vegetables. Bring to a boil, cover, and simmer 1 hour. Cool chicken in broth. Remove meat, discarding skin and bones, and set aside. Stir evaporated milk into broth and simmer 5 minutes. Place chicken in a 1½-quart loaf pan and pour broth and vegetables over top. Refrigerate overnight, slice, and serve. Portions can be frozen for later use.

1/4 cup dry bread crumbs
3 cups lean ground lamb, cooked
1 1/2 cups rice, cooked
3 tomatoes, chopped
2 eggs, lightly beaten

Lamb Loaf Bedlington

The Bedlington terrier's trim gives it the look of a lamb, but this dog is very much a terrier and was originally used to catch vermin and rabbits.

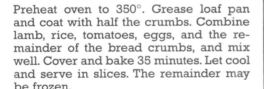

Preheat oven to 350°. Grease loaf pan and coat with half the crumbs. Combine lamb, rice, tomatoes, eggs, and the remainder of the bread crumbs, and mix well. Cover and bake 35 minutes. Let cool and serve in slices. The remainder may be frozen.

Did you know . . . ? Bedlington terriers often suffer from a hereditary condition commonly called copper toxicosis, which occurs when copper accumulates in the liver at toxic levels. Other breeds that can be affected are West Highland white terriers, Doberman pinschers, and cocker spaniels.

43

Portuguese Cod-Potato Bake

In many island or seafaring countries, such as Japan and the Scandinavian nations, fish is a staple in canine diets. And in Portugal, the duties of the Portuguese water dog included using his sense of smell to find schools of fish and "herding" fish into nets. A fish dinner was his usual reward.

butter for greasing

1 large potato, pierced and microwaved on each side for 4 minutes

8 ounces plain yogurt

8 ounces cod, cubed

1 14¹/₂-ounce can chopped tomatoes

Hint

Minerals are present in the body in only tiny amounts, but without them a dog's body couldn't do a lot of things, from forming bones and teeth to maintaining proper fluid balances. Nutritionists don't know the exact mineral needs of dogs, but studies have shown that dogs need calcium, copper, iodine, iron, magnesium, phosphorus, potassium, sodium and zinc. They also appear to need chloride, selenium and a number of other minerals. Because so little is known about the mineral needs of dogs, it's not a good idea to add mineral supplements to their diets.

Preheat oven to 350°. Butter a large baking dish. Slice potato and layer slices on bottom of dish. Cover with half the yogurt. Top with cod, remainder of yogurt, and tomatoes. Bake 45 minutes. Let cool and serve.

1 tablespoon canola oil

1 clove garlic, chopped

7 to 8 chicken livers

1 14½-ounce can chopped tomatoes

1 cup rice

2 cups water

Just Dandie Dirty Rice

The Dandie Dinmont terrier is named after a character in *Guy Mannering*, a Sir Walter Scott novel. These long little dogs were once known as pepper and mustard terriers after their coloring, which may be mustard (pale fawn to rich tan, with a creamy topknot) or pepper (pale silver to deep bluish black with a silvery white topknot).

Hint

Heat oil in skillet, and sauté garlic 5 minutes. Add chicken livers, tomatoes, rice, and water. Bring to a simmer, cover, and cook over low heat 20 minutes, until rice is done. Let cool and serve.

Do not feed any of these meals in excess. Use common sense in deciding how often to feed a homemade treat or meal and how much to serve. A tablespoon is an adequate serving for a Chihuahua, while a Great Dane may eat a one-cup serving.

Beef Borzoi

The borzoi, a large, longhaired sight hound, was used to course wolves in its homeland of Russia, where it went by the name Russian wolfhound. Its exotic appearance made it an impressive royal gift. Today, commoners too can enjoy the company of this elegant dog, as long as they can provide it with the amount of exercise and food it needs.

1 tablespoon vegetable oil

2 cloves garlic, chopped

1 pound lean ground beef (you may substitute ground turkey if you wish)

4 cups water

1 8-ounce package egg noodles

1 cup plain yogurt

Hint

Fat and cholesterol do not cause heart disease in healthy dogs, but obesity is the cause of many health problems.

Heat vegetable oil in pot, and sauté garlic 5 minutes. Add beef and brown. Then add water and simmer, uncovered, 15 minutes. Stir in uncooked noodles and cook, covered, 10 minutes. Remove from heat and let cool. Just before serving, add yogurt and mix well.

Holidays

CHAPTER 7

NEW YEAR'S DAY

2 strips bacon

1 can black-eyed peas, drained and
    rinsed, or 1 10-ounce package frozen
    black-eyed peas

$\frac{1}{2}$ cup long-grain rice, uncooked

1 cup water

Hoppin' John

Ensure your dog a healthy, prosperous year by feeding this Southern good-luck dish first thing on New Year's Day. It should be the first thing you eat, too!

Dice bacon and fry in a skillet. Add black-eyed peas, rice, and water. Cover and simmer over low heat 20 to 25 minutes. Cool and serve.

Hint

Be sure your dog has access to fresh, clean water at all times. Water evaporates quickly in summer's heat and freezes in winter's cold. Check your dog's water every day to ensure that it is drinkable and bug-free.

EASTER

1 10-ounce package frozen chopped
   spinach, thawed, drained, and
   squeezed dry
2 egg whites
2 cloves garlic, chopped
1/2 pound ground round or low-fat
   ground beef (ground turkey or
   chicken may be substituted)
1/2 cup instant brown rice
1/2 cup water
Lowfat or nonfat cream cheese
Food coloring to tint cream cheese

Spike's Spinach Meatballs

Your dog won't want to chase the bunny
that delivers these "eggs": He'll be too
busy eating. These healthy meatballs
are high in protein, vitamin A, B vitamins, magnesium, and zinc.

Mix spinach, egg whites, garlic, and
meat. Stir brown rice into simmering
water. When rice absorbs the water, add
to the spinach-meat mixture. Mix ingredients well. Form into egg-shaped meatballs appropriate for your dog's size
and arrange in a shallow baking dish.
To microwave: Cover and cook on high
for six minutes, rotating once; drain
well; cover and cook on high until no
pink remains in the meatballs and the
rice is tender. To cook in a conventional
oven: Bake at 350° 15 to 18 minutes; remove from oven and let cool. Soften
cream cheese and tint as desired with
food coloring. Use this "frosting" to dec-
orate the meatballs. Store in refrigerator. Serving size: one to two meatballs
per dog.

Easter Eggstravaganza

To get into the spirit of things, have an Easter egg hunt. Take plastic Easter eggs, fill each one with a meatball or small dog biscuit, and hide them around the house or yard. Then let your dog go to it! If your dog doesn't know the "go find" command, let him watch you hide the eggs and then help him search. He should get the idea pretty quickly. If your dog has had tracking training, this game of hide-and-seek will be a fun exercise for him.

INDEPENDENCE

DAY

Although they are omnivores, meaning they can survive on a variety of foods, dogs love meat. For a special Fourth of July treat, let your dog share in the festivities by serving him the following meal. Don't forget to reduce the amount of his regular dog food by the amount served here.

Hamburger

Make a patty with 2 to 4 ounces of lean hamburger meat (don't add any salt); the amount used depends on your dog's size. Grill until well done, and serve. Skip the bun and condiments; your dog doesn't need the extra calories.

1 cup of the dog's regular dry food

1 cup sliced strawberries

$^1/_2$ cup plain yogurt

Layer dry food, strawberries, and yogurt in the dog's dish and serve.

Strawberry Shortcake

Holiday Hints

Dogs can be frightened by the loud noise of firecrackers. The Fourth is not a day on which you should leave your dog alone in the yard or off his leash in an unconfined area. Every year, hundreds of dogs are lost when they run away from the flash and noise of fireworks.

Don't assume that dogs need the same amount of food year-round. Rather than basing the amount you feed on what the bag recommends, judge your dog's needs by how he looks and acts. Add or subtract food as needed depending on the weather (the dog may need more food in winter if he spends a lot of time outdoors, for instance) and the dog's weight and activity level. The dog's appetite may decrease during warm weather, especially if he is less active. Other dogs play hard in summer and may need more food.

HALLOWEEN

butter for greasing
3 eggs
1½ cups canned pumpkin
½ cup brown sugar
1 tablespoon cornstarch
1 teaspoon cinnamon
½ teaspoon ginger
¼ teaspoon ground cloves
¼ teaspoon nutmeg
1½ cups milk

Preheat oven to 350° and butter a l-quart baking dish. Break eggs into mixing bowl and beat. Add remaining ingredients, except for milk, and stir well. Scald milk and add to pumpkin mixture. Pour into baking dish, and bake uncovered 45 minutes. Let cool and serve. Store in refrigerator.

Papillon Pumpkin Custard

Keep Halloween candy out of your dog's reach, or you'll end up with one sick puppy. Instead, let your dog share in the festivities by serving this special treat at Halloween. If your dog is overweight and shouldn't have treats, add plain canned pumpkin to his meal. Pumpkin tastes good, is low in calories, and the fiber it contains helps fill dogs up.

Hint

Adult dogs don't tolerate lactose well, although small amounts (no more than 5 percent of the diet), especially if cooked, usually won't cause problems. You can also substitute rice or soy milk in any recipe calling for milk.

Tricks and Treats—Bobbing for Biscuits

Remember bobbing for apples when you were a kid? Why not let your dogs in on the fun? For an unusual entertainment at your next Halloween party, let your dogs bob for biscuits.

Holiday Hint

Some dogs are frightened by costumed trick-or-treaters coming to the door. If your dog becomes anxious or aggressive, confine him to a quiet part of the house until the fun is over.

To set up the competition, you'll need a water-filled container that is 18 to 20 inches in diameter, a platform for the dogs to stand on if the container is too high, a stopwatch or other timing method, and four biscuits per dog. With someone holding the first dog, drop the biscuits into the water and give a signal to begin, starting the clock at the same time. The object is for the dog to eat as many biscuits as he can within a predetermined time limit, usually 30 seconds to 1 minute. Verbal encouragement is okay, but no other help from spectators is allowed. The dog that eats the most biscuits in the allotted time is the winner. Be sure to practice beforehand so the dogs know what is expected. This is a fun birthday party game, too.

THANKSGIVING

Great Giblet Biscuits

Holiday Hint

Don't forget Fidough in the hustle and bustle of holiday preparations. Set aside some giblets to make him this special holiday treat.

1 cup chicken or turkey giblets
1 envelope active dry yeast
1/2 cup warm water
1/2 teaspoon sugar
10 ounces chicken broth, warm
3 1/2 cups all-purpose flour
1 cup whole-wheat flour
2 cups wheat cereal, crushed
1/2 cup powdered milk

Preheat oven to 300°. Cook and chop giblets. Cool. Dissolve yeast in warm water (about 110°) and sugar. Let stand 5 minutes. Add warm broth. In a large mixing bowl, combine remaining ingredients, plus giblets. Add yeast mixture and stir well. Roll out dough to 1/2-inch thickness and cut in desired shapes. Bake on greased cookie sheet 40 to 45 minutes. Turn oven off and leave biscuits to dry. Serve the same day or store in freezer.

There's nothing wrong with including your dog in holiday celebrations, but it's important to remember that his digestive system is smaller and more sensitive than your own. The holidays can quickly turn from fun to frantic if a dog overdoses on turkey and all the trimmings. Too much rich, fatty food leads to a common—and serious—disorder called pancreatitis. To avoid pancreatitis, permit your dog to have only tiny amounts of holiday foods, proportional to the dog's size. A tablespoon of turkey and dressing may not seem like much to you, but your beagle is much smaller than you are. Keep a tight lid on the trash, too. Those tempting aromas wafting from the garbage can are often too much for even a well-behaved dog to resist, but the poultry bones, chocolate, and fatty trimmings therein can be fatal treats.

CHRISTMAS

Staffordshire Steak and Kidney Pie

Have a Victorian-style Christmas Eve dinner with this delicious meat pie. It's rich, so serve it sparingly. (You'll want the rest for yourself!) Before bedtime, be sure you and Rover leave a biscuit out for Santa's Samoyed, who helps him herd the reindeer.

1 cup kidney fat, diced
1 beef kidney, trimmed of fat and diced
1 pound stew beef, diced
3 cups hot water
$1/2$ cup all-purpose flour, browned
$1/2$ cup cold water
pastry for two-crust pie

Holiday Hint

If your dog is still a curious puppy or has never learned to curb his habit of chewing anything and everything, take special precautions with holiday decorations. Tinsel, strings of lights, and toxic plants such as mistletoe and holly can all cause problems—intestinal blockage, electrical shock, vomiting, and diarrhea. To prevent an untrained dog from getting into serious trouble, confine him away from the Christmas tree and other holiday preparations when you can't be there to supervise. A wire or plastic crate, portable pen, or puppy gate is one of the most important safety items a pet owner can have, especially during the holidays.

Preheat oven to 400°. Melt kidney fat, and add diced kidney and beef. Brown over high heat 2 minutes. Add hot water and bring to a boil. Cover and simmer until meat is tender. Make a paste by stirring browned flour into cold water. Stir into stew until thickened. Line pie plate or casserole dish with pastry, and top with stew. Cover with second crust. Prick the top so the steam can escape. Bake until crust is brown. Let cool and serve.

BIRTHDAY

Birthday parties for dogs are nothing new. In his memoir *My Dog Skip,* Willie Morris describes a 1940s birthday party for his dog: "On his fourth birthday, [Rivers] even gave a party for [Skip] in her backyard, inviting a dozen or so of the neighborhood dogs and their owners. The trees and shrubs were festooned with colorful balloons and ribbons, and from her kitchen she brought out a birthday cake consisting of separate layers of ground meat and bologna in the approximate shape of Skip himself, with four candles on top and the inscription *Happy Birthday, Old Skip!* written meticulously in salted peanuts. We all sang 'Happy Birthday' to him, and then Rivers put the cake on the ground for the honoree and the other dogs. That cake was gone in about forty-five seconds."

3 pounds ground turkey
2 eggs (or 3 egg whites)
1½ cups oatmeal
2 teaspoons garlic powder
¼ cup parsley, minced
Low-fat or nonfat cream cheese
Food coloring to tint cream cheese

Preheat oven to 350°. Mix turkey, eggs, oatmeal, garlic powder, and parsley thoroughly, and mold into desired shape. You can go with the traditional round or square look, or get creative and go with a bone or tree shape. Bake on a broiler pan or on a rack over a cookie sheet 45 minutes to 1 hour and 15 minutes, depending on the cake's thickness. When done, remove from the oven and cool. Soften cream cheese and tint as desired with food coloring. Frost cake with tinted cream cheese. If you want to serve individual "pupcakes," cut out shapes with a cookie cutter before baking.

Bowser's Birthday Cake

Things haven't changed much. Fifty years later, the members of a Santa Rosa, California, canine play group called the Breakfast Club make this birthday cake as a special treat for their dogs. Member Anna Estep started the tradition. Reduce the recipe by half if you are serving only a small number of dogs.

Training with Treats

Using positive reinforcement—treats and praise—you can begin training your puppy when it is as young as eight weeks old. Training treats should be small, strongly scented, and easy to chew; you don't want to have to wait several minutes for your pup to finish a large biscuit, for instance. The best food treats to use include small slices of hot dog or Vienna sausage, cubes of cheese, liver bits, or even pieces of kibble.

To begin training, put several treats in your pocket and call your puppy to you. When he comes running, reward him with a treat. This puts your puppy on notice that good things are coming his way, and you're involved. (Get in the habit of keeping treats on hand, so you can reward your puppy whenever he is behaving appropriately.)

Basic Obedience

There are four commands every dog should know by heart: sit, down, stay, and come. Here, they are described as being taught to a puppy, but dogs of any age can learn these commands with the same techniques. The sit command is easiest to teach, so begin with that.

Sit

Call your puppy to you or go to him. When you have his complete attention, hold a treat above his nose and move your hand back, parallel to the floor. As he looks up at the treat, your pup should move naturally into a sit. As he sits, say "Sit" in a happy tone of voice. This helps the pup put a name to what you are asking him to do. As soon as the pup sits successfully, reward him with happy praise—"Good sit!"—and the treat. Praise should always come with or before the treat. Remember that puppies have extremely short attention spans. Keep words of praise short—"Good!" or

"Okay!"—so you don't confuse or distract your puppy.

When they are first learning to sit, young puppies will pop right back up, but that's okay. Your primary objective at this stage is to teach the puppy what you want and that good things happen when you're around. Practice the sit command several times a day for only a few minutes at a time. You don't want your puppy to get bored, and you don't want to stuff him with too many treats! (Don't forget to reduce the amount of your puppy's regular meals by the amount of treats given during training sessions.)

You can use your puppy's food dish in the same way to get him to sit at mealtimes. Sitting before meals is a good habit to teach. It prevents dogs from jumping up on people with food, and it teaches them to respect you as the food giver.

As your puppy becomes more proficient at this command, begin rewarding him for responding to your voice command only, without any guidance. Then start reducing the number of times you reward him for complying. Your pup should never be sure when a reward is coming. Eventually, he will sit in response to your voice command or hand signal only, and your praise will be sufficient reward.

Down

This command is more difficult to teach, but it's an important one for your dog to know. The down command reinforces your position of authority and comes in handy when your dog is visiting the veterinarian or groomer or must be examined by you at home.

As your puppy is sitting, hold the treat beneath his nose and slowly move it toward the floor between his front paws and then in front of him. Your pup should naturally lie down as he follows the path of the treat. (Never force your puppy into any position; you could hurt him and you will take all the fun out of the learning process.) As the pup moves into position, say "Down" so he can put a name to the command. As with the sit command, reward with praise and a treat the minute the pup succeeds. Again, your pup will remain down for only a short time, but as he grows older and more proficient, you can increase the amount of time you require him to stay down.

Stay

When your pup is familiar with the down command, add the stay command. Teach this while the pup is wearing a leash so you can enforce your request. Using a treat, lure the puppy into the down position. Reward him for complying, and then place your foot on the leash close to the latch and stand up.

Your puppy will try to stand, too, but will be unable because the leash is so short. As he lies back down, say "Stay." Follow the same praise/reward schedule described above. Once your dog has learned all three of these commands, you can combine the sit and down commands with the stay command.

Come

This is the most important command your puppy will ever learn. It has saved the life of many a dog who was about to run in front of a car or was running headlong toward some other danger. Teach your dog to turn tail and come instantly when you call.

Begin by rattling a box of treats or making some other sound that is sure to get your dog's attention. When he runs to you, praise him and give him a treat. Once he is doing this reliably, combine his name with the command: "Sounder, come!" To finish off this command, put your puppy on a twenty- to thirty-foot clothesline. (This gives the puppy the illusion of freedom but allows you to reinforce the command even at a distance.) Holding one end of the line, tell the dog to sit and stay, and then back away from him. When you are some distance away, say "Come." As he comes toward you, keep backing up and taking up the slack in the line. (If he doesn't respond to the come command, pull on the line to give him the right idea.) When he gets to you, praise him wildly and give him a treat. Practice with the clothesline until you are sure your dog will come reliably. Then do some off-leash practice. Stay in an enclosed area until he has this command letter-perfect.

Teaching Tricks

When your dog knows the basics, you can start teaching him more complicated tricks, building on what he already knows. Here are two easy tricks you can teach.

The Crawl

This trick is easy to teach once your dog learns the down and come commands. Begin by putting your dog in the down position. With a treat cupped in your hand, kneel a few feet in front of her, say her name, and then say "Come; crawl." This phrase links the command your dog knows—come—with a new one—crawl. Hold the treat in front of her nose and slowly pull it toward you. If your dog tries to stand to get the treat, correct her, put her back in position, and repeat the command. Give her the treat once she performs correctly, even if she moves only a short distance. Gradually increase the distance she must crawl to get the treat.

Roll Over

Your dog must know the down command to learn this trick. Place him in the down position. Kneeling in front of him and using a treat to entice him, encourage him to lie on his side, saying "Side" as he moves into position. Accompany the side command with a hand signal—an open palm moving in the direction (left or right) you want your dog to lie. If you want the dog to lie on his right side, use your left hand, and vice versa. Repeat this step frequently until you are sure your dog knows what to do. Next, introduce the roll command both verbally and with a hand signal—a slow, complete circle with your hand (holding a treat, of course). As he looks up to follow the course of the treat, help him roll over and then give him the treat. Again, practice this step frequently until your dog is rolling over on command without your help. After completing the roll, he should be back in the down position. Once Rover has this sequence down pat, you can teach him to roll back in the other direction.

Good as Golden Liver Squares

From the *Retriever Believer* newsletter comes this recipe for a treat most dogs can't resist: liver bites! Keep them on hand for training sessions, or use as bait in the show ring.

1 carton liver
2 eggs
1 teaspoon garlic powder
1 cup cornmeal
1 cup wheat germ
½ cup powdered milk

The golden retriever was developed in England in the mid to late nineteenth century by Sir Dudley Marjoribanks, Lord Tweedmouth, who preferred retrievers with yellow coloring. With a flat-coat retriever as a foundation, he built the golden with crosses to tweed water spaniels (now extinct), Labradors, a red setter, and wavy-coated retrievers.

Preheat oven to 325°, and grease cookie sheet. Combine liver, eggs, and garlic powder in blender, and blend until smooth. Combine dry ingredients in bowl, then add blended ingredients and mix well. Spread mixture on cookie sheet, about ¼ inch thick. Bake 20 minutes. Cool and cut into small squares. Keep frozen.

Ban Begging

This habit may seem cute when a puppy is young, but it quickly becomes annoying. Your best bet is to prevent it altogether. To ensure that your dog develops the best canine manners and would be welcome at any table set by Emily Post, set firm ground rules from the beginning. Don't reward begging behavior. Never feed your dog at the table or allow him to sniff around the table while the family is eating. Instead, require the dog to go lie down in another area or to lie quietly at the table. Be sure that all family members and guests follow the rules.

Good Pup Pie

The recipe for this special pie comes from *The Scoop*, a newsletter on training.

Take 1 puppy, roll and play with him until slightly pampered, and add the following ingredients:

1 cup patience
1 cup understanding
1 pinch correction
1 cup hard work
2 cups praise
1½ cups fun

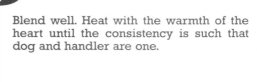

Blend well. Heat with the warmth of the heart until the consistency is such that dog and handler are one.

*Putting Your Dog
on a Diet*

CHAPTER 9

Obesity is the single most common nutritional problem to plague dogs. Veterinarians report that up to 25 percent of the dogs in their practices are overweight, which is defined as being 10 to 20 percent or more over normal weight. Obesity can shorten a dog's lifespan and results in higher veterinary costs, because it contributes to disease and injury such as heart, lung, and skeletal problems; a higher risk of diabetes, liver, and kidney problems; increased anesthetic and surgical risk; increased likelihood of hip dysplasia and other skeletal disorders; and greater risk of heatstroke. Keeping your dog at a healthy weight is healthy for your wallet, too!

Why are so many dogs fat? For one thing, their food tastes better than ever. Commercial food manufacturers offer a variety of flavors designed to appeal not only to a dog's taste buds but also to owner perceptions of what dogs like.

Along with palatability, the practice of free feeding contributes to obesity. Few dogs will regulate the amount they eat. If you set out unlimited food, assuming that your dog will eat only as much as he needs, you are likely to end up with a fat dog. The canine brain is hardwired to direct the body to take in food when it is available, because in their wild past, dogs never knew where their next meal was coming from. Of course, that's not the case today for most dogs, but the brain's programming has not yet caught up with modern realities.

Another fact of modern life is the two-earner household. Today's dog owners have less time to exercise their dogs, but they still feed their pets the maximum amount of food recommended on the bag or can. Too many treats or table scraps are another cause of obesity.

Neutering does not cause obesity, but it is usually done at a time in the dog's life when its growth rate and energy needs are decreasing; thus, the correlation. Just like people, dogs get fat because they eat too much and don't exercise enough.

Obesity can have some medical causes, such as hypothyroidism, which occurs when the thyroid gland doesn't produce enough thyroid hormone, thus slowing the dog's metabolic rate. Fat dogs should be examined by a veterinarian to ensure that their obesity doesn't have a medical cause. If the dog doesn't have a health problem, your veterinarian can suggest an appropriate diet, as well as an appropriate weight-loss schedule. The dog should not lose weight too rapidly, nor should he be put on a strenuous exercise program. Exercise and weight loss should be done gradually. As the dog's condition improves, he can exercise more frequently and for longer periods.

Is Your Dog Fat?

Fat dogs waddle when they walk. They develop fatty areas over the hips and at the base of the tail as well as around the face, neck, and shoulders. Fat dogs are inactive or tire easily after only mild exertion. Respiratory difficulty such as panting heavily after a short walk or going up stairs is common.

It's easy to give your dog the hands-on test to determine if he is overweight. A dog's ribs should not be visible (if they are, the dog is too thin), but they should be easily felt through a layer of skin, subcutaneous tissue, and muscle. A dog who is too fat has a slight to heavy covering of fat over his ribs. Fat deposits may be noticeable at the base of the tail or, in grossly obese dogs, around the neck and limbs.

Preventing Obesity

Diet and exercise are complementary;

neither can be successful without the other. To control a dog's weight, you must provide appropriate amounts of food and exercise. Severely obese dogs may need to eat a specially formulated weight-reduction diet. In most cases, however, you can either reduce the amount of the dog's regular food or feed the dog a low-fat diet that allows him to eat the same amount he is used to getting.

Whether to feed less food or to feed a low-fat diet depends primarily on your attitude toward food. If you equate food with love and would find it difficult to feed less, you may find it easier to give your dog the same amount of a low-calorie diet than to feed less of the dog's regular diet. If you choose to feed less of your dog's regular food, you may be concerned that your dog will feel deprived. A good way to help the dog still feel full after receiving less food is to mix the food with canned pumpkin, which is low in calories but high in fiber. Its taste is appealing to the dog, and the fiber will help him feel full. Other low-calorie treats include fruit, vegetables, and plain rice cakes.

Stop obesity before it starts by establishing a routine and sticking to it. Regular exercise and mealtimes are frequently recommended to human dieters, and they work just as well for dogs. A scheduled walk or jog is something your dog will learn to anticipate as special time with you. The same goes for mealtime. Instead of free-feeding, offer your dog's meals at set hours. He will learn not to expect food at any other time.

If your dog is sedentary and prone to weight gain, ask your veterinarian to recommend an appropriate food for weight loss. And scrap the table scraps, which are often high in fat and calories.

(Instead, prepare some of the healthy, low-calorie treats in this book.) Don't be tricked by "puppy-dog eyes." Begging should be discouraged, and all family members should agree not to feed the dog except at regular mealtimes. Everyone must understand and agree to the need for weight loss, or the dog's diet can be sabotaged. To decide if your dog needs to lose weight, take the following quiz:

1. **How much exercise does your dog receive daily?**
   a. He walks from his bed to his food dish and back again, plus two-minute morning and evening trips to the backyard.
   b. He walks one block with you to and from the school bus stop to meet the kids.
   c. The two of you take a brisk twenty-minute walk in the park daily.
   d. His name is Yukon King, and he was the lead dog of this year's winning Iditarod team.

2. **What is your dog's physical condition?**
   a. His waist disappeared years ago, and he waddles when he walks. It's an effort for him to stand up.
   b. If you press really hard, you think you can feel some ribs.
   c. You can run your hands along Rover's side and feel his ribs underneath a layer of muscle. He has a visible waist when viewed from above and an obvious abdominal tuck.
   d. Rover has abs of steel and is the mascot at the local gym.

3. **Is your dog gaining weight?**

a. When Tank walks through the house, you stop what you're doing to wonder if a truck has driven by or if an earthquake is happening.

b. When friends say they didn't realize Beagles were so large, you airily reply, "Oh, he's really big for his breed."

c. You have studied your breed's standard, and his weight is right on the money.

If you reply more often with *a* or *b* answers than *c* or *d* answers, you need to consider adjusting the amount of activity and food your dog receives. Ask your veterinarian to help you set up an exercise and diet plan.

Treats and homemade meals should not comprise more than 5 to 10 percent of a dog's diet. Whenever a dog receives treats or home-cooked meals, his dog food should be decreased by the appropriate amount. Don't fool yourself by thinking that a little bit won't hurt. Remember that what seems like a small amount to you can be excessive for your toy poodle or beagle.

Exercise Is Important

CHAPTER 10

Take frequent walks in the neighborhood. If you and your dog are athletic, regular hikes, jogging, or bicycling are good ways for the two of you to burn calories. Never assume that your dog will exercise himself in the backyard. Like people, dogs require motivation to exercise; left to themselves they will become couch potatoes, develop destructive tendencies such as chewing inappropriate items, or develop behavior problems related to their pent-up energy.

Before beginning an exercise program, take your dog to the veterinarian for a complete checkup. Certain types of exercise may not be appropriate for puppies, whose skeletal structure is still developing, and middle-aged dogs may need to begin slowly and work up to a regular exercise program. Just as people who exercise too violently without being in shape develop sore muscles, so do dogs. Your veterinarian can check for intestinal parasites, heartworms, other cardiovascular anomalies, and overall condition, all of which can affect a dog's ability to run, jump, or take long hikes.

The image of roly-poly puppies is common, but it is not healthy. Rapid growth during puppyhood, related to excessive calorie and calcium intake, contributes to development of orthopedic disease such as hip dysplasia. Ensure your puppy's healthy growth by not letting him gain weight too quickly. Ask your veterinarian how much weight your puppy should be gaining, and weigh him on a regular basis.

To reduce your dog's weight, feed less food (reduce the amount by 20 to 30 percent) or feed the dog a high-fiber, low-fat food. Feed smaller, more frequent meals to ease hunger pangs. Don't give junk food.

Active Dogs

Just because a dog is young or plays hard with the kids doesn't mean it needs a high-energy food. Such a diet should be reserved for dogs that consistently work at a job or sport such as hunting, weight pulling, or sleddog racing. Show dogs, which travel frequently and are under the stress of competition, and pregnant or lactating bitches can also benefit from energy-rich foods. These dogs need the extra calories found in high-fat, high-protein diets.

Power-Packed Peanut Butter Cookies

These cookies are very high in protein. Take them along as energy boosters on hikes or camping trips.

¹/₄ cup shortening
¹/₂ cup peanut butter
¹/₄ cup brown sugar
1 egg
¹/₂ cup wheat germ
3 tablespoons water
³/₄ cup whole-wheat flour
¹/₄ cup soy flour
¹/₂ cup powdered milk

Preheat oven to 375°. Combine shortening, peanut butter, sugar, and egg, and mix well until smooth. Stir in wheat germ and water. Combine and add flours and powdered milk. Roll into 1-inch balls and place on greased cookie sheet. Bake 8 minutes. Let cool and serve.

1/2 cup peanut butter
1/2 cup honey
1 cup powdered milk
1 cup rolled oats
1/2 cup wheat germ

High-Protein Peanut Butter–Honey Balls

These, too, are good sources of energy for the active dog, and they are easy to pack along whether you and your dog are jogging at the beach or hiking the Appalachian Trail. Both of you will enjoy them.

Combine first four ingredients and mix well. Form into balls (1 teaspoon for toy breeds, 2 teaspoons for medium-size dogs, and 1 tablespoon for large dogs) and roll in wheat germ to coat. Serve. Refrigerate leftovers.

Getting Your Dog in Shape

Condition your dog gradually. Don't just assume that your dog is in shape to go on a three-mile run without any preparation. Like people, dogs can get sore or sprained muscles from exercising too strenuously, especially when their bodies aren't ready for it.

It's also important that the dog have the appropriate physical build for the sport or exercise you have in mind. A bulldog is not a good jogging partner, and a dachshund can injure its back playing Frisbee. A Labrador retriever or a greyhound makes a great jogging partner, but a short-legged basset hound probably won't be able to keep pace.

Ask your veterinarian to examine your dog before introducing him to any kind of strenuous exercise, especially if your dog is less than two years old or more than five years old. Puppies are still growing, and certain forms of exercise can inhibit skeletal formation or cause injuries.

Be sure the two of you warm up before you begin an activity and cool down when you are finished. During summer, exercise early in the morning or after the heat of the day. Too much exertion in hot weather can cause heat exhaustion or heatstroke, characterized by loud, raspy, rapid breathing and gums that have turned purple or gray. If you see these signs in your dog, get him to a veterinarian immediately. Hot asphalt can burn a dog's paw pads, so be sure his feet are protected with booties if it's necessary to venture out in midday.

Food-Related Disorders

The canine brain is hardwired to search out food, and with its sensitive nose and Houdini-like ability to go places it isn't allowed, the dog is well-equipped to meet this challenge. Unfortunately, the canine willingness to eat anything and everything can be its downfall. A number of food-related disorders can affect dogs, from diarrhea to salmonella poisoning. Fortunately, however, most such dietary disasters are easy to prevent by watching how and what your dog eats, as well as monitoring its access to trash and other forbidden items. Following are a few of the conditions that can affect dogs. Some are related to the ingestion of a particular food, while others are indicated by a change in appetite.

Biotin Deficiency

Biotin, a B complex vitamin, is found in yeast, liver, and egg yolk. A biotin deficiency occurs when a dog eats too much raw egg white. For this reason, as well as to avoid salmonella poisoning, never feed raw eggs.

Bloat

Gastric dilatation volvulus, or bloat, occurs when the stomach rotates, closing off its openings and leaving air and fluids unable to escape. The pressure cuts off blood circulation, and the stomach tissues begin to die. Technically, bloat is not caused by diet, but most dogs that bloat have just eaten a big meal, followed by drinking large amounts of water or exercising strenuously. Commonly affected breeds include basset hounds, bloodhounds, Doberman pinschers, German shepherds, Great Danes, Irish setters, and Saint Bernards.

Signs of bloat include a hard, distended, hollow-sounding abdomen, belching, dry heaves, increased salivation, and depression. A dog with bloat may frequently lie down and get up, whine, pace, or stretch. If you suspect bloat, rush the dog to a veterinarian, even if it's the middle of the night. Immediate treatment—which usually requires surgery—can mean the difference between life or death.

To prevent this potentially fatal condition, large, deep-chested dogs should be fed small quantities of food several times per day rather than a single large meal. Limit the amount of water the dog drinks immediately after eating, and make sure he rests for one hour before and two hours after each meal. Once bloat has occurred, it is more likely to recur unless the veterinarian performs a surgery called a permanent abdominal wall gastropexy.

Chocolate Toxicosis

Chocolate and Valentine's Day go together like wine and roses, but chocolate and dogs can be a sickly—and sometimes lethal—combination. The theobromine in chocolate is toxic to dogs and can cause vomiting, increased urination, hyperactivity, an increased heart rate, diarrhea, panting, tremors, seizures, and coma. Unsweetened baking chocolate contains the highest amount of theobromine and thus is most toxic, but a dog that devours a box of chocolate candy is likely to be pretty sick, too. Dogs are known to have a sweet tooth, so save your dog and your carpet by keeping any form of chocolate out of reach.

If your dog does scarf up a box of chocolate, treat the situation as an emergency. Your veterinarian may need to induce vomiting to reduce absorption of the chocolate into the bloodstream.

Dental Disease

Cavities aren't common in dogs, but

periodontal disease is. It occurs most frequently in dogs that eat primarily a canned or semi-moist diet. The residue from food forms a soft film of bacteria-filled mucus on the teeth called plaque. Plaque hardens into tartar, or calculus. Tartar buildup causes bad breath, loose teeth, and even serious organ infections. To help scrape tartar off teeth, be sure your dog has a supply of abrasive treats such as hard biscuits or access to dry food. Daily or weekly brushing is the best way to prevent dental disease.

Diarrhea

From poisons to parasites, disease to diet, loose or liquid stools can have a number of causes. Most commonly, however, the culprit is dietary. A dog can get diarrhea from eating inappropriate table scraps, getting into garbage, eating nonfood items such as feathers, or eating too much of any food, even its regular diet. A rapid or unexpected change in diet can also bring on diarrhea.

When a dog develops diarrhea with no other symptoms, withhold its food for twenty-four hours. Then feed a bland meal of equal amounts of boiled chicken and rice. If the runny stools continue for more than forty-eight hours, your veterinarian should examine the dog. Severe diarrhea can cause dehydration, and it is a common sign of intestinal disease, so it should not be ignored.

Fatty Acid Deficiency

Fatty acid deficiencies are rare, but they can occur. A dog whose diet is deficient in fatty acids may have a coat that is dry, dull, or coarse; dandruff; or thickened skin. Overall, his condition is poor. If you think your dog's diet is lacking in fatty acids, ask your veterinarian to recommend an appropriate food or supplement. No controlled studies on fatty acid supplementation have been done on animals, so benefits and amounts of supplementation are not clear.

Food Allergy

Food allergies are not common in dogs, but when they occur they can be caused by reactions to certain proteins such as beef and chicken, dyes or preservatives, or to common food ingredients such as wheat, corn, and milk. Signs of food allergy include vomiting; skin that is red, irritated, or itchy; diarrhea; and abdominal pain.

If your veterinarian suspects a food allergy, he or she may recommend putting your dog on what is called an elimination diet, or hypoallergenic diet. This involves feeding the dog a commercial or homemade food to which it has not previously been exposed. Formerly this meant feeding the dog a lamb and rice diet, but today those ingredients are found in many dog foods. Now commercially made hypoallergenic foods contain such uncommon ingredients as rabbit, venison, turkey, fish, potatoes, and barley. Whether it is commercial or homemade, the diet must contain ingredients that your dog has never eaten before. To ensure that this is the case, read the label on your dog's old food and compare it to the ingredients in the hypoallergenic diet. It's also important to eliminate treats and rawhides while the dog is eating the hypoallergenic diet.

After the dog has been on this diet long enough to resolve the signs (up to three months), new foods can be added one at a time to determine which ones the dog is allergic to. When allergenic foods are identified, they should be eliminated from the dog's diet.

Nutritional Secondary Hyperparathyroidism

Dogs that eat all-meat diets or home-made diets that are improperly formulated may develop a condition called nutritional secondary hyperparathyroidism (NSH), caused by either a calcium deficiency or an improper ratio of calcium to phosphorus. NSH is easily avoided by feeding a complete, balanced food.

Pancreatitis

The pancreas produces digestive enzymes that break down fats so the body can use them. When there is too much fat in the body, the pancreas works too hard and becomes inflamed. The result is intense abdominal pain, lack of appetite, and a loose, fatty stool. If pancreatitis is not recognized and treated, the dog can die. This condition is most common in middle-aged, overweight female dogs, but dogs of any age, size, or sex can develop pancreatitis.

Protein Deficiency

Because there are so many good commercial foods available in pet stores and grocery stores, protein deficiencies are uncommon. However, they can occur when generic foods or improperly formulated homemade foods are fed, or when a dog is given a diet that is inappropriate for its lifestyle or age. Signs of protein deficiency are lack of appetite with corresponding weight loss, a rough, dull coat, and poor growth. If your dog has these problems, don't try to solve a dietary deficiency by randomly switching foods. Discuss the situation with your veterinarian, and ask her to recommend a more appropriate diet. If the switch to a food with high-quality protein and high digestibility doesn't help, your veterinarian may refer you to a veterinary nutritionist.

Salmonella Poisoning

It is wise to assume that raw eggs and poultry are infected with salmonella bacteria, according to a USDA publication. These bacteria can cause food poisoning and gastrointestinal inflammation, so you should never feed your dog raw eggs or raw meat or poultry, no matter how "natural" a diet it may seem.

Salmonella poisoning is a zoonosis, meaning it can be transmitted not only to other dogs but also to humans. Wash your hands frequently if you are dealing with a dog with salmonella poisoning, and clean the dog's food and water dishes after each use.

Salmon Poisoning

This canine gastrointestinal illness occurs only in the Pacific Northwest. It is caused by rickettsial bacteria found in raw salmon. Salmon poisoning is easy to prevent: Don't feed your dog raw salmon. Hikers, hunters, and fishermen who take their dogs into Idaho, Oregon, Washington, and British Columbia wilderness areas should take care that their dogs don't eat any dead salmon found washed up on river banks or beaches.

Skeletal Disorders

Too much of anything can be harmful, and this is just as true of nutrients as it is of anything else. Fast-growing puppies are prone to a number of skeletal disorders, including hip dysplasia, osteochondrosis dissecans, and osteochondritis. These bone malformations are most common in large- and giant-breed dogs who grow too rapidly.

Excess nutrition is one of the factors

that can cause these diseases; other factors are environment and heredity. A common cause of skeletal disorders is too much calcium. Because commercial foods already contain high amounts of calcium, adding calcium supplements to a dog's diet can throw the balance out of whack. It's better to improve quality of food than to experiment with supplements and risk a puppy's health and high veterinary bills. If you feed a homemade diet, ask your veterinarian to consult a veterinary nutritionist to determine how much calcium your growing puppy needs.

Skin Disease

Poor coat and skin quality are common signs of nutritional deficiency. A dull, dry, brittle coat; hair loss; and flaky, greasy skin can be signs that a dog's food is not doing its job. Other skin-related signs of nutritional deficiencies are thickened nose and paw pads; fading coat color; and itchy skin. When itching is severe, dogs scratch constantly. The abrasions caused by scratching can result in bacterial skin infections.

The best way to ensure a shiny, healthy coat and skin is to feed a high-quality food that is complete and balanced. Some skin problems can be caused by deficiencies of fatty acids or zinc, but other vitamin or mineral deficiencies are rare, especially if the dog eats a well-balanced diet. Listed below are some common nutritional problems that result from improper diet. Most of them are easy to avoid by feeding a high-quality, properly formulated commercial or homemade diet.

Vitamin A Toxicity

Vitamin A is a fat-soluble vitamin, so it builds up quickly in the body and becomes toxic. It should never be added to